HOW TO LAND YOUR DREAM INTERNSHIP

Tam Pham

"After landing six different internships and working at his college's career center, Tam Pham is an expert at landing internships. This book easily trumps all internship advice I've ever seen. It's a thorough A-Z guide to helping you start your career before you're thrown into the real world."

—Matt Tran,
founder of Engineered Truth

"Tam Pham hits it out of the park again with a comprehensive, hard-hitting, truthful, and insightful approach in *How to Land Your Dream Internship*. With a combination of insights from his first bestseller, *How To Network*, and new additions from his own internship experience, this is the book for new graduates looking to break in. Get this book and don't look back."

—Albert Qian,
founder of Albert's List

"Tam showed us the ropes on *How To Network* with his last book, masterfully if I may add. Well, he's at it again, but this time he's rocking the internship world and turning all other career guides out there upside down. This (ultimate) blueprint is comprehensive to the point that it will leave one competent, confident, and excuseless. Read for yourself and you'll find that you'll have no reason left for you to be unable to land your dream internship."

—Evan Pham,
Performance Marketer at Growth Pilots

"Tam's guide has helped me subconsciously put myself in the right mindset, and ultimately, land me my dream internship at DreamWorks. He takes all the seemingly obvious job search tips (from resume building to interviewing to simply having the right attitude in approaching everything), and quite literally walks you through it step by step in application. I felt like Tam was my own personal coach and cheerleader, all in one. This guide gave me a definite plan of action, and helped me tremendously in getting where I am right now."

—Rebecca Wang,
student at University of Southern California

"I spoke with Tam a little over a year ago when he first offered career guidance. I was an incoming college freshman so I really did not know where to start or what direction to take. However, I did know that I wanted to be able to do more than just go to school and go home and, ultimately, that

I wanted to land an internship by summer time. Tam taught me how to structure my resume, develop my professional profile, and how to properly network. Working with Tam, it wasn't hard to recognize his passion for helping others succeed, and he does it in a way that's easy to understand and take in, removing a lot of the unnecessary frustration that comes with internship hunting. Tam is a great friend and mentor who really knows what he is talking about and I strongly believe that those who wish to jumpstart their professional careers should look to Tam."

—Nam Vu, student at San Jose
State University

"Tam's guide has helped me become more confident with networking and talking to all sorts of people. I'm no longer afraid of making that first move to get an internship that can benefit me for the rest of my life."

—Amanda Huynh, student at UC
Santa Barbara

"Tam knows that it takes more than just a flawless resume and standard interview skills to land an internship. He gave me the belief and confidence in myself that I needed to get the ball rolling on my career!"

—Shelley Tan,
student at UC Irvine

"*How To Land Your Dream Internship* opened a world of opportunities for me! These days, navigating the world of internships can be difficult if you don't know where to look. Tam's book not only helps you pinpoint what kind of internship you want, it also primes you to become the best candidate for the job. Following the steps outlined in this book will not only guarantee that you will land your dream internship, it will teach you essential business skills that you will utilize throughout your career.

—Jessa Parayno,
student at San Jose State University

"This book needs more pictures."

—Eric Pham,
5th grade student at Norwood Creek Elementary

HOW TO LAND YOUR
DREAM
INTERNSHIP

Proven Step-By-Step System
To Gain Real World Experience

Tam Pham

CONTENTS

PART ONE

INTRODUCTION

Landing an internship today is unnecessarily complicated and time-consuming. We've been taught the "right" way to approach our job search is to submit our resumes to 50+ different job sites, cross our fingers, and pray for a response (which usually never happens).

Why does this never work?

We've been listening to the wrong advice from adults who don't understand how to job hunt in the 21st century. This book will show you how to land your dream internship in a proven and systematic way. *How To Land Your Dream Internship* is designed for the busy young person (like you) to achieve your career goals without the frustration.

Before I dive deep into the different strategies, I'll share a little introduction about myself. My name is Tam and I'm a normal dude from San Jose, California. My life seriously changed for the better when I did internships in college.

I went from being a lost and confused freshman into a man (Mom thinks that's debatable) who finally has an idea of what he really wants to do in life. With internships, I've gained so many different skills, pushed myself out of my comfort zone, and made life-long friends throughout.

I also had many failures. For example, I never heard back from 50+ companies when I applied to my first internship. I've bombed countless job interviews.

I even forgot my name once while introducing myself to an employer at a job fair.

Not fun.

I had to learn the hard way on how to land internships. Now that I've been around the block a fair amount of times, it is my turn to help YOU be more successful than me.

I've personally landed six different internships, mentored dozens of college students, and worked at my university's career center before turning 21. There was no clear and easy to read internship guide out there so I wrote this book out of necessity.

This book ain't full of theory. It's raw, actionable, and full of advice that has already been tested with several students. The young people I've mentored have gone on to intern for creative companies like DreamWorks, reputable companies like Facebook, and startups across San Francisco.

This book is right for you if:

- You are a motivated and ambitious young person

- You want to advance your life and your professional career

- You want to gain real experience in the field that you're interested in

This book is probably not for you if:

- You are looking for a quick and easy way to be "successful"

- You are a person who loves sucking up information but never takes action

- You are not open to new or unconventional approaches in the job hunting world

Still interested? Good.

Don't be the person who misses out on advancing their career by wasting time with outdated advice. I'm giving you the exact blueprint I wish I had when I was 18 so you don't have to make the same mistakes as I did. Take control of your life right now, land your dream internship, and enjoy the new life you're now creating.

Okay, that was a little bit corny. I apologize.

I'll show you every step in your journey. Read this with an open mind and before we get started, I want to invite you to join my insider's list if you haven't joined already.

Go to **OutsideOfTheClassroom.com/InternshipBonus**, and enter your name and email.

You'll get exclusive updates on this book, internship opportunities, and a curated list of articles and books every week to help you on your journey. You'll also get direct access to me so I can answer any questions you might have while reading the book. Say hi!

After you join the club, let's dive in.

HOW INTERNSHIPS WORK

Bigger Picture: Here's how the real world (typically) works.

You graduate high school. You go to college. You take on massive student loan debt. You get a degree. You struggle to find a good high-paying job. You end up working a low-paying job you are overqualified for.

You get mad. Frustrated that no one better would hire you. Or offer you a higher salary. You complain. In the meantime, your student loan debt is collecting interest. You're upset at this cruel world for not paying you for what you deserve. You seek help from a career counselor.

You ask them, "Why are all my job offers so bad?"

They'll ask you, "Have you done any internships in college?"

"No."

"Oh, that's why."

How do I know this? I have many friends who have gone through the exact situation. While working at my university's career center, recent graduates seek help for EXACTLY this reason.

To quote Slate Magazine,

"Today's crop of new B.A.s are staring at roughly 8.5 percent unemployment, 16.8 percent underemployment. Close to half of those who land work won't

immediately find a job that requires their degree, and for those stuck in that situation, there are fewer 'good' jobs to go around. Welcome to adulthood."

Employers are reluctant to hire these new graduates because they have no real world experience. This is where internships come in.

First, let us define: What is an internship?

The dictionary definition is *"a temporary position with an emphasis on on-the-job training rather than merely employment, and it can be paid or unpaid."*

More simply, an internship is working for a company to gain real world experience.

Why are internships important?

- Internships help you get your first foot in the door to make getting a full-time job easier.

- Internships let you learn more about yourself and what you really want to do in life.

- Internships are pretty fun when you are doing work you enjoy with awesome people.

- Internships give you exposure to how the workplace functions.

- Internships allow you to meet like-minded people in your field, including future mentors and friends.

HOW DO INTERNSHIPS WORK?

Typically, you intern for a company.

A company may hire an intern to take some of the workload off their full-time employees. The full-time employees can then focus their energy on the more high-skilled or important work. But don't think of an intern's job as "dirty work." This means as an intern, you do work that is relevant in your field so that you can hone your skills and gain real-world experience.

Companies hire you as an intern to help out in a specific area they are lacking.

A company may want you as an intern to strengthen different departments like their struggling social media team, a company rebrand, or marketing to student groups.

Internships have a time restriction.

Internships typically range from three months to a year, but it all depends on the employer's needs and bandwidth.

Internships can be paid or unpaid.

Due to national labor laws, unpaid internships are technically considered "illegal." But many companies violate this law.

When an intern agrees to work "for free", it is most likely because they see the huge value they will receive in return regardless of money (or they're desperate for experience and the company is being cheap as hell).

Unpaid internships are most common with startups and local businesses and less common with established companies.

Should you consider doing an unpaid internship?

My short answer: ONLY do an unpaid internship if it is an opportunity you simply cannot pass up.

If you're a basketball player and had to choose between a paid position at the YMCA Basketball Summer Camp or working an unpaid position for NBA legend Kobe Bryant, which opportunity would you choose?

The answer is obvious.

Working with Kobe Bryant will help you learn faster, be surrounded by world class athletes, and will probably be more fun.

If my dream job was to be a Marketing Manager at Google, I would take an unpaid marketing internship at Google in a heartbeat. In the long run, that position in Google would best help me achieve my goals and make me happier.

Ask yourself: Where would you be able to learn and grow the most?

Note: I dislike unpaid internships because not everyone can literally afford to take the position. Some students have to work and provide for their family. Unpaid internships take away the opportunity to make money at a different job therefore making you have to choose... or work two jobs. Unpaid internships threaten those who cannot afford to work for free and benefit the rich. Isn't society great?

One internship leads to the next.

For anyone to take you seriously after college, you need to prove yourself. With internships, you can show to your future employers that you have the skills and work experience that will add value to their company.

For me, it was all a domino effect. I luckily landed one interview with a big name company as a college freshman after applying through my university's job board. The interview went well and I got the job. When I applied for my next internship, they noticed my previous internship experience and they hired me solely because of that! And for my third internship, fourth, and so on.

From a company's perspective, they're thinking, "If these other big companies hired him, he must be talented!" My first internship built my credibility and opened magical doors for me. I'm confident that it will open doors for you, too.

I found out I hated what I "thought" was my dream job.

When I interned for a big name company, I thought I was the shit. I had my own cubicle, my own phone, and even my own work email. Our cafe had the best food and they even gave me a badge to access any building I wanted. It felt just like what I saw in the movies.

But the work I did drained me, emotionally and mentally. Not because my work was super difficult, but because it was work that I did not enjoy. I thought I would love to do administrative work, but this internship taught me how much I never wanted to be "trapped" in a cubicle crunching numbers on a spreadsheet ever again.

Doing internships was my wakeup call and made me question, **what do I really want in life?**

Imagine if I never did an internship. I would have stayed on the business track for four years and ended up working a low-paying job that I would have grown to hate. And when I finally realized I wanted to switch careers, I would have had to start from square one again in a totally different industry at age 23 while still in debt.

Internships provide realizations and experiences that you won't gain in a classroom. You never know if you really want to pursue something until you try it out!

I met amazing people!

Even when my internships ended, I still kept in touch with my former co-workers, both interns and full-time employees.

It's so great to surround yourself with like-minded people. Other interns are people who are just like you: ambitious, eager to learn, and awesome to be around. In the future, your friends can also refer you to new opportunities and invite you to cool events.

There's a reason why business professionals emphasize how *"your network is your net worth."*

I gained skills that are actually useful.

Although my first internship can be seen as a bust, I learned some pretty neat skills.

I became a pretty FAST file organizer. I learned the secret on how to walk to the cafe, eat lunch, and walk back in under 30 minutes. I learned how to drive in the carpool lane without getting caught (bad tip).

But in all seriousness, I learned new skills at every single one of my internships, good and bad. This made me more valuable to every company I interned for because the more problems you can solve with your skills, the higher chance companies will be fighting to hire you.

I learned skills to help me to start a business.

It's difficult to start a restaurant if you never worked for a restaurant.

If you've ever had an idea of starting a company, you HAVE to intern and work for someone else. You'll understand concepts like culture, organizational skills, and leadership. *These are skills many first-time startup founders often lack.*

I know not everyone reading this wants to start their own business, so I'll end it here.

It's all about the Benjamin's and perks!

I actually made good money making $13 / hr during my first internship and enjoying the company's cafe, basketball court, and other awesome perks. Of course you're not supposed to join a company solely for the bonuses, but they sure are attractive.

Key Takeaways:

- Don't be another college graduate who can't find jobs after school. Do internships.

- Internships can be paid or unpaid. It is up to you to decide on what position you want to take. Do internships.

- Internships are awesome for many different reasons. Do internships!

Actions:

- Read the next chapter.

CHOOSE YOURSELF

~⌐

Bigger Picture:

Before you begin your internship search, you need to be clear on what you want.

I believe this is the most important chapter out of the whole book.

Now I know what you're thinking...

"Tam, I don't care what internship position I get. I just want something under my belt so I can build my resume. Just show me how to do it, god damn it!!"

Honestly, this was EXACTLY what I was thinking when I looked for my first internship. But I learned the hard way that this is the exact opposite mindset you should have.

Before my internship experience, I thought I wanted to do administrative work behind a cubicle. I thought I would love working with spreadsheets and organizing files. But I was miserable during my first internship. I quit within five months (stayed that long partly for the cafe) and told myself how I would never do that work ever again.

This first step is the most crucial one.

If you don't know what YOU want to learn, what YOU want to explore, what YOU want... You end up wasting a lot of your precious time.

For example:

If you want do social work... DO NOT TRY TO GET AN INTERNSHIP IN ACCOUNTING.

If you are majoring in psychology, DO NOT TRY AND GET A JOB IN CONSTRUCTION.

If you want to go into the medical field, DO NOT OFFER TO WRITE FOR YOUR LOCAL NEWS STATION.

This sounds simple, but you wouldn't believe how many people take positions JUST to put it on their resume. It is infuriating.

Investor Warren Buffet said it best,

"There comes a time when you ought to start doing what you want. Take a job that you love. You will jump out of bed in the morning. I think you are out of your mind if you keep taking jobs that you don't like because you think it will look good on your resume. Isn't that a little like saving up sex for your old age?"

You need to FOCUS! You want to take internships so that you can grow and explore your field. What if you don't know exactly what you want to do? That is what this "Choose Yourself" chapter is all about, and I have two recommendations:

1. Online Research

2. Informational Interviews

Let's start with the former.

Online Research:

Go on Google and search about your field and the different jobs that can come out of it.

- Search: [Field of Study] Internship Job Description

- Search: What career options are there for [Field of Study]

- Search: People who graduated with a [Field of Study] Degree

- Visit TheMuse.com and use their exploration feature.

- Visit CareerPlanner.com where they can "match" you up with different career choices based on your personality.

Have a baby's mind and simply explore! You can also find communities for more curated answers.

Online Communities:

- Reddit.com: Search for your specific subreddit (topic) to find the latest posts about your specific field.

Warning: Don't go overboard and get lost while reading. It is easy to get hopelessly distracted on Reddit!

- Quora.com: Quora is like Reddit without the anonymity. I personally like Quora for their vibrant community and high-quality answers.
- Glassdoor.com: You can find information like: CEO approval ratings, salary reports, interview reviews and questions, benefits reviews, office photos and more.

The point of online research is to find potential positions that you want to learn more about. We are NOT deciding on one job yet, we are simply exploring our curiosity.

Informational Interviews:

The second (and more direct) option for career exploration is to **talk to real people who have been there before!**

Informational interviews are conversations with people who are in the position you aspire to be in. The point is to learn more about their position and seek advice. Someone who has been in your shoes before can tell you exactly what to expect. You can then be the judge to decide whether it would be a path worth exploring.

I once had an informational interview with an investment banker and he described how stressful the 80 hour work weeks were and how much of his work dealt with analyzing numbers. I was instantly turned off. That helped me realize how much I did not want to go into finance.

If I did not have that 15 minute informational interview, I would have busted my butt trying to get an internship at financial company, Morgan Stanley, only to hate it after two weeks.

Think about the bigger picture. What do you really want?

A small amount of time spent here will save you a massive amount of time later down the road.

Another big bonus with informational interviews: Not all jobs are advertised, but those on the inside may be knowledgeable about current or future job openings.

There's a common phrase given to entrepreneurs when they're trying to raise capital from investors: *"When you ask for money, you get advice. When you ask for advice, you get money."*

Not always true but when you ask for a job, you get advice. When you ask for advice, you may get a job opportunity.

Who should you interview?

- Professionals who are working in your "dream job" position

- Hiring managers in the specific company you want to work for

- Previous interns who have worked for that company or your position

What questions should you ask them?

Insightful questions can be:

1. I've noticed that you graduated from [School] and worked at [Company A] and [Company B]. What made you want to go into [Field] in the first place?

2. What is your day-to-day like?

3. What are some of the best and worst parts about your position?

4. How is the company culture compared to your previous company?

5. What is a typical career path for this position?

6. My strongest skills are in X, Y, and Z. How do you think I can use these skills to fit into the organization?

7. What traits, skills, or experiences do employers in your field look for in candidates?

8. Is there something you wish you had known or a skill you wish you'd had starting out in [this field]? Anything you wish you had done differently starting out?

9. If you were me, an eager student looking for an internship, what would you say is the best way to get my foot in the door?

10. Is there anyone else who you think I should speak to?

These questions are just to start. Once the conversation flows, more questions will naturally come to mind because you will begin to get more curious.

Remember, the informational interview is NOT about asking for a job.

It is purely for learning purposes. It helps you understand more about the position and see if it is a path you want to pursue. Ask any questions that will satisfy your curiosity about the position.

Where should you have the informational interview at?

Wherever the interviewee feels comfortable.

Informational interviews are usually done at the interviewee's office or at a cafe close to them. Remember, they are sacrificing their time to help you. The least you can do is offer to meet wherever is convenient for them.

(Yes, you should offer to pay for their coffee/lunch. Since you are a young person, they probably won't let you, but always offer. Kindness goes a long way.)

Informational interviews work best in person but Skype or phone interviews are healthy alternatives. If the person you're trying to meet with is really busy, ask if you can send them a few questions via email instead.

How should you prepare for an informational interview?

You have to respect their. The interviewee is taking 10-30 minutes out of their day to speak to you. There's very little to no benefit for them to help you so please come prepared.

- Do your homework. Research everything you can about them and their past work experience.

- Have your questions ready. Don't waste time asking questions about them that you can easily find online.

- Bring a pen and notebook. Be ready to take notes!

- Bring a watch to keep track of time. Don't rush the conversation, of course, but don't overstay your welcome.

- Whatever you do, do NOT ask for a job.

How should you find people to do an informational interview?

I'll go over many different ways to find professionals to interview and let you decide what is best for your situation.

- **Ask people who you know (my favorite and most effective avenue)**

Ask friends if they know anyone who you can interview. If they know you're serious, they should be more than happy to introduce you to someone!

Here is a general script you can use (change it however you like):

"Hey [Name]! I hope all is well.

I am curious to learn more about [Field of Study] and the different career paths it entails. Do you know anyone in [Field of Study] that I can have a 15-minute chat with?

I would really appreciate the connection, thanks in advance. :)"

- **Facebook (Or any social network)**

Go to Facebook. Seriously. Post a status saying,

"Hey friends! I genuinely want to learn more about [Field of Study]. Do you know anyone in [Field of Study]) that I can have a 15-minute chat with?

I would really appreciate the connection, thanks in advance. :)"

The world is small. Everyone knows somebody who knows somebody (who knows somebody) who fits your demographic.

• Facebook Groups

No friends? No problem.

There are a ton of Facebook groups for all different purposes, including internships. Search for local internship groups and post on there.

• LinkedIn

LinkedIn is a "Facebook for professionals." We'll talk about why LinkedIn is important and how you HAVE to sign up later. But I wanted to quickly share how to find people through this social platform.

Instead of posting in groups and passively waiting, you can go straight to the source. If you wanted to have an informational interview with a Finance Manager, you can type "Finance Manager" on the LinkedIn search bar and see all the possible results.

Next, you can "Connect" (like a Facebook friend request) with that person and send them a message asking for an informational interview. You'd be surprised how eager professionals are willing to help out a student if you just ask.

If they decline your request, don't sweat it. Thank them and move on. There are plenty of other people who would be willing to help you out.

• LinkedIn Groups

Similarly to Facebook groups, there are several LinkedIn groups you can join. It is also a great place to find more candidates to personally reach out to.

- **Cold Email**

Emailing someone directly can be highly effective when you do it correctly.

Once you have their email (Google "how to find someone's email"), briefly introduce yourself and politely ask them for a 15 minute chat using the scripts above.

For your subject line, you can write something simple like,

Subject Line #1) May I interview you for 15 minutes?

Subject Line #2) Love your work. May I ask you for some advice?

Subject Line #3) I'm a Junior at [SCHOOL]. May I ask you about your career?

- **Meetup groups**

If you want to learn more about marketing, find the events where marketing professionals go to and talk to them.

You can use websites like Meetup.com or Eventbrite.com to find local and professional events. When they ask you, "What do you do?" or "What brings you here?", you can tell them how you are a business student who's eager to learn more about marketing. Then ask, "Do you mind if I ask you a few quick questions about what you do?"

Be mindful of their time and remember that you did not schedule any appointment with them.

Ask your most important questions. Be brief. Thank them, take their business card, and move on to the next person. After the event, thank them again through email. Offer to help out in any way that you can. Keep in touch!

- **Clubs and Organizations**

In high school and college, there are organizations that have plenty of connections to professionals. Most of the time, these connections consist of college alumni or former club members.

Reach out to the club officers and ask for an introduction. Join the organization if you want to be involved. You can also meet other students who have interned in your field of study before.

- **Professors**

Your professors can be a great source for advice and may even know someone who would hire you. Reach out and share what you're curious about and ask if they have any advice on your situation.

During the Interview:

After you find someone to interview and you have your questions ready, how should you act? A few basic pointers:

- Look in their eyes (seriously) and simply listen. It should be 90% of them talking and 10% of you responding to their answers.

- Take notes. If something is not clear, politely bring it up and ask for clarity.

- Did I mention not to ask for a job?

Reflection:

After going through a few informational interviews, here are some questions you should ask yourself:

- Do you have a better understanding of your major? Interests? Passions?

- Do you have a better understanding of what you want to learn?

- Do you have a better understanding of what type of company you would want to work for? (Established company, startup, local business, etc.)

- Think back to your informational interview when you asked the interviewee what they did on their job. Are those the same responsibilities that you hope to fulfill in the future?

- Have you learned enough about how to get your foot in the door?

- Now will you take their advice and actually do it?

Note: The more informational interviews you do, the more clarity you will have. Don't just think one is "good enough." Five is a good number. The more perspectives you see, the more educated your decision will be.

After the interview:

Send them a thank you email showing your appreciation for their time. A week later, find a way to give back and help them. This could be sharing an article that might be useful to them or an opportunity that they should be aware of.

Two weeks later, email them again telling them how you have used their advice and share the results that have happened because of it. They will LOVE you for this!

This email tells them that you're serious about your career, which gives them more reasons to help you out in the future. Keep these relationships close and always find ways to be helpful. You've made a new friend and learned more about your career. How awesome is that?

Conclusion:

Please don't skip this step. You need to know what you want to learn and what your goals are before you aimlessly start your job hunt. Don't do any future steps until you have a better understanding of what your internship goal is, trust me.

Key Takeaways:

- You have to know what you want. Clarity comes with curiosity and action!

- Discover different positions through online research and informational interviews.

- Informational interviews are awesome learning experiences and gives you a competitive edge in networking.

Action:

- Spend at least 30 minutes researching your field online, every day for the next week.

- Find five people to have an informational interview with. Do whatever it takes (legally).

- Follow up with everyone you meet and keep them updated on your journey.

PART TWO

PREPARATION

Bigger picture: Now that you know what kind of internship you want, it's time to prepare everything you need to make it happen.

The following chapters will cover exactly everything you need to know before you actually go out and search for internships. **Warning: this will take work.** Just because you have the blueprint does not mean you'll actually get your dream internship.

Let's dive in.

What do you need for your job search?

You need a resume, cover letter, and a stellar personal brand. Let's get started.

RESUME

~

Jobsearch.com defined a resume as "a written compilation of your education, work experience, credentials, and accomplishments that is used to apply for jobs."

In my voice: A resume show employers who you are and what you have accomplished in your professional career. It is the bare minimum of what you need to get a job.

Many people get caught up in the little details like how big the font size should be or how to format the resume. Don't worry about all of that for now. Let's focus on the high level goals of your resume first.

Realize that you are marketing yourself.

For example with music, Taylor Swift is the product. When she is marketing her album, she is actually marketing herself. When you are marketing your skills and experiences, you are actually marketing yourself. You are the product. How can we make your product (you) appealing for the customer (recruiter) so they can buy (hire) you?

Tell YOUR story!

Your resume needs to paint a clear picture to the employer about you and your experiences.

If you want show how much of a technical nerd you are, write your resume in the language that will make you look like a technical nerd. If you want to show how you're a finance geek, write your resume in the language that will make you look like a finance geek. If you want to show your passion for filmmaking, write your resume in the language that will highlight your film experiences.

Entrepreneur Sydney Liu told me that after speaking to hundreds of college recruiters, the biggest problem they face is that students' resumes all look and sound the same.

"They have the same projects, same courses, same college. Same everything. How can you be DIFFERENT?"

Liu advises students to emphasize the experiences that make you unique. Your projects. Your special skills. Your story. YOU.

Focus on your strengths, not your weaknesses.

If you have a low GPA, don't sweat. Showcase your work experience and projects more than your GPA. If you don't much have work experience, emphasize your GPA, courses, and projects.

After you understand these basic principles, let's dig in on how to actually create your resume.

Create a Resume

You could create one by scratch, but why do the hard work? I recommend the following sites:

1. https://standardresume.co/ (My favorite)

2. http://ineedaresu.me/

3. http://creddle.io/

4. https://www.cakeresume.com/

5. https://represent.io/

Your resume should have the basic necessities:

- Name

- Email

- Website

- Education

- Work Experience

- Skills

- Projects

- Extracurriculars

There is no "perfect" way to structure a resume and I don't care what your teacher, mentor, or ex-boyfriend says. Just remember to paint a clear story about how your experiences and skills can help the company.

Education

On top of including your major and graduation date, include relevant coursework. Think about it. If you just put "San Jose State University: Bachelor Degree in Psychology," they can assume your expertise is in many things.

But if you listed your coursework in a more specific way like this:

- 107B. Studies in Gender and Sexuality

- 109. Topics in Race, Ethnicity, Gender, and Sexuality Studies

- 165B. Gender, Sexuality, and Body, 1700 to 1850

You are actually painting a story for the recruiter to see what you're actually interested in and how it may relate to the job you're applying for.

Include your GPA if it is over a 3.0. If you're still in school, the school section should be at the top. If you're out of school, prioritize your work experience.

Work Experience

This is the MOST IMPORTANT section in your whole resume.

You want to do your best to quantify and express your work experience as vividly as possible. There are many ways to explain yourself but here is an easy formula you can refer to in case you get stuck.

Action X => Measured by Y => By doing Z

For example:

- Spearheaded planning for the Global Studies' commencement ceremony of over 512 attendees by leading my student organization.

- Provided organizational support to over 50 staff members including managing schedules, supply purchasing, filing, preparing development materials, and coordinating meetings.

- Improved access to health care services for 80 qualifying community members by planning monthly team meetings with lawyers, physicians, and social workers to efficiently process approvals.

You don't have to use this formula for EVERY point but it provides you with a good foundation to get started. Then you can edit your points to make it sound more natural.

A few tips when filling your work experience in:

Recruiters LOVE numbers / statistics

Use real numbers to paint a picture on your impact with any project or work you've done. How many people were in attendance at the event you hosted? How many impressions did you receive on your marketing campaign? By how much percent did you improve from last year's numbers?

Showcase your passions

If you are a YouTube partner and are getting paid from advertisers... you can definitely include that experience on there (if it's relevant to what you're applying for). You're a freaking Content Creator! Or if you're a blogger and average 10,000 unique visitors a month, that's amazing! You can brand yourself as a content creator, writer, and even a marketer.

It all depends on what your career goal is so if it's relevant, share what you're up to outside of the classroom.

Projects

Projects can be things like a video you had to create, a business competition you participated in, or an app that you made in your spare time.

Projects are an opportunity to show that on top of your work experience, you are different because of *these reasons*. Show your personality. Tell a story about yourself with the work you're passionate about.

Extracurriculars

What clubs or organizations were you involved in? What did you do within those extracurricular activities? Were you in a leadership role? What were some of your responsibilities?

Be proud of what the activities you are involved in and paint the picture of how your presence elevated the organization.

Skills

What special skills do you have that can benefit the company? Are you good at editing videos? Content marketing? Event planning?

Stop this book right now and go create a first draft of your resume. Add a few sentences and bullet points to the categories I labeled earlier.

Don't focus on perfection. Focus on completion.

The first draft is always ugly. Just do it and we can worry about "optimizing" it later.

*

*

*

*

*

Done? Good.

The main questions you should be asking yourself:

- Did you tell your story? How are you different?

- Did you paint a clear picture of your experiences?

- Did you show the value you can give to their company?

Everyone's first draft will always be far from perfect. If you want inspiration, check out these resume samples: https://www.visualcv.com/resume-samples

Notice the different formatting, styles, and designs. Find what you like about each one and what you dislike. Write them down. Now how can you paint a clearer picture of yourself? There is no "right" answer. But focus on doing whatever it takes for your resume to paint a clear picture about your experiences.

After you fix up your draft, read through the questions below to avoid common resume errors.

Should I make my resume one page?

Yes.

Should I list dates of my previous work positions?

Yes.

Should I have an objective statement?

No. If you are applying for a marketing internship, you don't need to say, "Objective: Looking to enhance my skills in the field of marketing." Well, no duh? Why else would you be applying? Cut this line and make room for more important things.

How should I structure my resume?

However you think it would make your experiences and story more clear.

What should my page margins be?

One inch on all sides.

Should I have a QR code scanner?

No.

Should I include pictures on my resume?

No.

Should I have my headshot on my resume?

No. (Seriously?)

Should I write at the bottom, "References available upon request"?

No. If they want references, they will ask you. Don't waste space.

Should I include my high school activities?

Generally, no. But if it's your first ever resume and you have nothing else, make it sound good.

What font should you use?

Times New Roman or Arial.

Should I have my resume in different translations?

No.

Should I proofread my resume?

Yes. Do it ten times. Then ask five friends to proofread it and give you feedback. Fix and improve.

Should I focus more on my projects or my work experience?

Focus on what makes YOU unique and what the employer would want in a candidate for that role.

If you're looking for a position in film, highlight your video projects over your barista experience. If you're looking for a position in marketing, highlight your experience marketing your club over your involvement with the chess club. Highlight the experiences that are most relevant for your job position.

Should I mention that I love Taco Bell?

Not unless you are applying for a Taco Bell internship.

Action: Spend the next hour and rewrite your resume. Look at other resumes for inspiration, go through the questions above, and make changes that you think would be best to paint your story.

Do this before moving on to the next step!

*

*

*

*

*

Done? Awesome.

When you apply for internships, the next step is to tailor your resume to fit the position you're applying for.

This step is like buying Christmas gifts for your friends. Do you think they will all love you for your $5 Starbucks gift card? Or would they love you more if you gave them a gift that was thoughtful and specific to them?

Like gifting Aziz Ansari's book, *Modern Romance*, to your friend who is obsessed about relationships. Or gifting a Magic Bullet to your cross fit loving vegan friend. Or giving tickets to a live stand-up performance to your comedy nerd friend.

The effects of tailoring your resume is massive.

How can you tailor your resume?

Read the company's job description and identify the words they frequently use along with the tone they wrote in. Can you make your resume sound exactly like what they're looking for?

For example, if a company says they're really looking for an organized and detail-oriented person to be their event manager, you can literally put under your "Skills" section:

- Organization

- Detail oriented

Or express these skills in your last job experience:

"Organized and executed the annual Fall Leadership Conference with over 3,000 attendees and received a 95% satisfactory response."

Do this step throughout your resume so that they know this resume is specific for them. Recruiters notice this and will reward you. Once you finish writing and tailoring your resume, share it with a few trusted friends and mentors for feedback.

COVER LETTER

In addition to a resume, create an awesome Cover Letter to go along with it. Jobsearch.com defines a cover letter a way to "provide the employer with additional information as to why you are a good candidate for the job."

In my voice: Don't just be like every average candidate submitting resumes. Go the extra mile and create a cover letter to further highlight your skills, especially in writing.

Like resumes, there is no perfect way to write cover letters. Based on my experience and research, here is a simple and easy format that can be used for any job.

Opening Paragraph:

Why are you writing?

Tell them where you found the job position, who the hell you are, and why you want the job in the first place. Simon Sinek, author of *Start With Why*, repeats frequently:

"People don't buy what you do, they buy why you do it."

People don't buy Apple products because they have the fastest software or the best memory storage. People buy Apple products because they believe in their mission of being different. Going against the status quo. Creating minimalist designs.

Going back to the cover letter, really stress WHY you want the position. Tell them a short story on why you're so passionate about that subject or what specifically you want to learn.

Start with WHY.

Paragraphs (2-3):

Highlight the best points from your tailored resume. Elaborate on how those specific experiences would make you a valuable asset to the company.

Do. Not. Restate. What. Your. Resume. Says.

Elaborate and go more in detail. You're writing to a human being. Don't treat the reader like a robot.

Closing Paragraph:

Ask for the interview. Politely thank them for their consideration and show how excited you are to hear back.

PERSONAL BRAND

One of the first things recruiters do before they hire you is look your name up on the Internet. Some people are afraid, but this is a good thing! You have another outlet to show how unique you are and how you understand the digital world.

Are you on LinkedIn? Do you have your own website? How are you on Instagram?

I met a student two weeks ago who changed her last name on Facebook so employers couldn't find her... Well, don't be afraid. You have nothing to hide. Right?

I talked to Thomas Frank, founder of CollegeInfoGeek.com, on my podcast and I picked his brain on personal branding. In a nutshell, Frank said it's making people recognize you as an expert in your field.

What do you want to be known as? The lazy and unmotivated student? Or someone who is curious to learn everything about [whatever you're studying here]?

Let's go step-by-step on how you can maximize your online presence and build a personal brand you will be proud of.

Join LinkedIn

LinkedIn is a "Facebook for Professionals" and the platform is used by over

300 million professionals globally. Yes, it's another social network but there are no risks to join (it's free) and comes with so many benefits:

- Highlight your work experience, volunteer work, and organizations you're in
- View other LinkedIn members (like the people who will interview you)
- Recruiters can find and possibly recruit you straight from LinkedIn
- Showcase your work by publishing blog posts on LinkedIn
- Highlight your skills and have members "endorse" you
- Establish, grow, and manage your network online
- People can leave public recommendations for you
- Great way to connect after meeting someone
- Avenue to ask for informational interviews
- Read news under the topics you follow
- Join groups that fit your interests

"LinkedIn is great for young people" – My mom

Okay Tam I get it, I need a LinkedIn profile. How do I get started?

Register at http://www.linkedin.com. Complete your profile to the best of your ability. LinkedIn has an easy on boarding process (just follow their steps).

This process should be smooth because you can simply copy what you've written on your resume and paste it on LinkedIn. I could go in depth with all the little details but the theme is clear: **This is your professional network, take it seriously.**

Your work experience, profile picture, and your status updates will be public and seen by professionals. Keep your drunk photos to yourself!

Update your LinkedIn profile to the fullest so that you have a "completed profile."

That includes:

1. Photo: A simple and clean headshot. Smiles encouraged :)

2. Headline: Tell the world what you're excited about. It can be as simple as saying "Grad Student At Ohio State University Looking For Marketing Internship Opportunities"

3. Summary: Describe who you are, what skills you have, and what opportunities you're looking for. KISS (Keep it simple, stupid).

4. Organizations: Highlight the clubs and organizations you were involved with. Show what you did within that organization.

5. Education: Where did you go to school? When are you graduating?

6. Skills: Add your top 5-10 skills and let your connections endorse you for what they think you're best at.

7. Honors and Awards: What awards did you have during school? Dean's Scholar? 1st Place in a business competition? Share it!

8. Courses: Show what classes you took that is most relevant to your goal. For example, if you want a marketing internship, highlight all the business and psychology courses you took.

9. Projects: Did you build an app? Create a video? Lead a group project?

10. Recommendations: Ask your classmates, co-workers, or professors who have worked with you to write a recommendation. This builds social proof and credibility to future employers looking at your profile.

Remember, we are not striving for perfection. We are striving for completion. This is a profile that is always changing so like a resume, don't stress yourself out. Done is better than nothing at this point. Now go make a LinkedIn account!

Clean all Social Media

This is funny because this tip seems so obvious but so many people DON'T get hired because of what they post online. Go on all your social media sites and take down inappropriate photos, videos, or anything that might be a red flag to an employer.

Create Your Own Personal Website

Everything is digital which means the old one sheet resume is never enough. Having an online showcase where you can vividly express your unique self is an option our parents never had.

With a website, you'll instantly be more impressive in the recruiter's eyes just because 90% of other applicants don't have one.

It'll make you stand out of the crowd, guaranteed. Take advantage of this golden opportunity! Here are some resources that I would recommend:

1. About.me: Drop dead simple landing page about yourself.

2. Strikingly.com: Build a beautiful mobile-friendly site in minutes.

3. Squarespace.com: Create a full-blown professional site, no code required.

4. Vizualize.me: Pulls info from your LinkedIn and creates a really cool infographic resume.

5. Wordpress.org: Wordpress hosts more than 20% of all websites online. A bit more complex but a worthwhile investment in my biased opinion.

In your website, make sure to include these key things:

1. About Me: This page is called "About Me" but it's really not about you. In this page, talk about how you will BENEFIT whoever hires you.

2. Resume: Upload a PDF file so employers can easily see what you've been up to.

3. Contact Page: Add your email and yes, you should make sure it's not the one you made in 6th grade.

Other things you may consider:

1. Portfolio: Show off your work in writing, graphic design, coding projects, etc.

2. Blog: Employers love applicants who know how to write, a skill that

is applicable in any field. Share your thoughts and it will definitely impress any online visitor.

3. Testimonials: If you have worked anywhere before, you can ask your co-workers for testimonials! This page will include quotes and photos of people you've worked with and this will increase your credibility. You can also pull this info from your LinkedIn recommendations.

4. Social Media: Since you have nothing to hide, be proud and show off your online presence on Twitter, Facebook & LinkedIn!

5. Press + Interviews: If you've been interviewed for the local news, school paper, or featured on your organization's website, this would be a great addition to build your credibility.

For inspiration, check out these personal websites that I love:

- Cassidy Williams: www.cassidoo.co

Right off the bat, you can clearly see who Cassidy is and what she does. A simple and effective website that highlights her work extremely well.

- Devon Stank: www.devonstank.com

Clear and beautifully designed. Devon does a great job on marketing his value and experiences.

- Rachel King: www.rachaelgking.com

This is probably my favorite because of how vividly Rachel shows her personality. It has less information compared to Devon and Cassidy's websites but this website alone proves how you don't have to be a "website expert" to create your online presence.

After you finish creating your website, ask for feedback from trusted friends. Add your website to your email signature so that when you send e-mails, anyone can learn more about you from your website!

This doesn't have to be complicated. A website alone makes you stand out of the crowd and if it is free (or at a super low cost), why not make the investment?

It's like lifting weights every day (job hunting) but your efforts are all gone to waste because of your bad nutrition (resume, cover letter, and website). You need both to succeed.

NEXT STEPS

The cover letter (or any of this stuff) isn't hard. There are systems and proven formulas that work. HR professionals and recruiters speak frequently at different events and universities sharing exactly what they look for in job candidates.

We are simply working backwards to achieve our desired results, trust the system. You're doing great.

Key Takeaways:

- A resume is important and it is the bare minimum. Make one.

- A cover letter complements, not restates, your resume. Make one.

- You need a LinkedIn profile. Complete it!

- Your online presence is important. Keep it clean and professional.

- Create your own website and stand out of the crowd.

- None of this is about perfection. It's all about taking that first step and being the best you can be today.

Action steps:

- Create a resume (30 minutes)

- Complete your LinkedIn Profile (20 minutes)

- Go through your social media and ask yourself, "If I was an employer, would I hire me?" Delete anything that might jeopardize your job search. (15 minutes)

- Build your personal website (30 minutes minimum)

- Do a simple Google search of your name and see what comes up. If there is anything you want to hide, delete it ASAP. *Pro tip: If you are on the fence on whether or not you should delete a picture, you should probably delete it.* (15 minutes)

- Get feedback on your resume, LinkedIn profile, and website from five trusted adults. Consider their suggestions and make improvements that would best emphasizes your unique experiences. (60 minutes)

The (times) are the minimum efforts you should put in. The more work you do (obviously), the better your chances of landing an internship.

PART THREE

ATTITUDE

~

I never intended to write this chapter but after working with so many young adults, I felt like this book wouldn't be complete without it.

I just want to tell you that you are great.

And I seriously mean that.

No, I'm not trying to be all motivational and corny. I truly mean that. During your job search, there may be times when you'll feel frustrated. For example:

- The HR representative never scheduled you in for a job interview.

- A person didn't email you back for an informational interview.

- The recruiter never got back to you after you submitted your application.

Or whatever.

It's not because they think you're inadequate or worthless. People could not get back to you for a variety of uncontrollable reasons. Don't sweat the small stuff.

Entrepreneur Seth Godin talks about how in every difficult journey, we go through "the dip" or the part where you will feel confused, lost, and hopeless. But those who become successful were the ones who, instead of hitting the dip and quitting, went back even harder and made it to the top.

In this process, don't give up. Be one of the special few that get past this dip.

You are great and don't let anyone tell you otherwise.

Let's move on.

JOB SEARCH

Now that you know what internship you want and have prepared accordingly, we are ready to move on.

There are many different ways to find internships. Countless ways. I'll go over each avenue, feature every resource I know, and share my personal experiences.

Bigger Picture: After reading all of the different avenues, you have to decide what is best for YOU. There is no one "right" way to find internships. Every avenue has its pros and cons.

I'll go over everything and give you my unbiased opinion. That being said, I will explicitly give you my biased opinion because some ways suck much more than others and I really, really, really, don't want you to waste your time.

Aren't you glad you have me?

The three methods to landing an internship are through the Front Door, Side Door, and with the Creative Approach.

FRONT DOOR

~⁓

This approach is the most commonly used route with students searching for internships. They find a random job site online, make a profile, submit a resume, and wait for a response.

Pros:

- Easy to apply

- Very convenient to view all the available jobs in one place

- Can apply to many positions at once (increasing efficiency)

Cons:

- Low success rate

- Lower quality jobs

- More competition

- Less opportunity to personalize

- Sometimes the employers have already found someone

The front door is like Tinder: high number of results, low yield.

There are multiple websites to go through the front door and I want to share with you the resources I personally know.

WayUp.com

WayUp is undoubtedly the BEST front door website.

I interviewed Nina Boyd, member of WayUp's founding team, about landing internships and the approach WayUp takes is pretty rad. Part of their application requires you to have short answers to specific questions, giving you more chances to show your personality directly to the employers. They have a high response rate with trusted employers and are rapidly dominating the college market.

I reached out to the founder Liz Wessel on how to best utilize WayUp, and she had one important comment:

> *"Make sure that you have a strong online presence... because the chances are that employers will Google you if they're even remotely interested in hiring you. At WayUp, every student who signs up gets an automatic public profile (which they can always opt-out of)... That profile can be found on Google by employers, which means that it's important for students to 'beef it up' (especially to avoid employers from finding your embarrassing Facebook pictures!)"*

You can sign up with my referral link at www.wayup.com/refer/tampham16 or without my affiliation at www.wayup.com. Regardless if you use my affiliate link, I respect my readers and want the best for you. I highly recommend this website.

Here are other websites that you can also explore. I personally don't use these websites, so I would highly recommend doing your due diligence.

- InternMatch.com

- CareerBuilder.com

- Internships.com

- Indeed.com

- Monster.com

- Craigslist.com

It's not that these options are bad, they're just so saturated. I would personally stay away and use WayUp.com or the different options that I'm about to explain.

School Job Boards

Most universities have a portal of job opportunities that are filled with local positions. This is a much better "front door" because the people who post on your school's job board are actually looking for candidates from your school. Therefore, when they get an applicant request from your university, they are expecting it and usually won't brush it off.

However, I understand not every school has a stellar career center (which is ironic because school is supposed to help you get a job). So take advantage of your career center if you have the opportunity and if not, don't sweat. There are a ton of other ways to get internships today that this book covers.

How do you succeed in the front door?

If you do decide to use the front door, here are a few tips to get you to the top.

• **Have a Tailored Resume**

Everyone is spamming their generic resumes and complaining they're getting no responses. Be different. Show the employer that you have done your homework and have taken that extra effort to impress them!

• **Quality over Quantity**

Do not spam your resumes. Pick a few quality positions you are really interested in, and put a lot more effort into those specific applications.

• **Strong Online Presence**

The first thing the recruiters will do is look you up online, keep your personal brand professional.

• **Follow Up**

Follow up with each company after 1 week of no response. Follow up again after 2 weeks of no response. Then 3 weeks.

After not hearing back, you have two main options: Apply for more jobs or stop using the front door. Front doors can work if the site is active and trusted (like WayUp), but be cautious of your time and energy.

SIDE DOOR

~

Think about the last expensive product you bought. Was it dinner at a fancy restaurant? New shoes? A MacBook? How did you find out about it? You most likely bought that product because it was recommended to you by somebody you trust. The same principles apply with employment.

I wanted a part-time job in high school and my friend Mia, who worked at Jamba Juice (think Starbucks, but for smoothies), told me that she can introduce me to her manager, Katrina.

After I came by the store to say hi, Katrina scheduled an interview and hired me the very next week. From a company's point of view, referrals make SO MUCH SENSE.

Imagine for a second that you are a manager. (Crazy, right?)

Imagine looking through 50 different applications from random teenagers, interviewing 10 of them, and then deciding to keep 2 for the team. The 2 people who you just hired seemed promising but turned out to be complete busts. You fire both of them. Now you're understaffed at the busiest time of the year (summer) and you have to start the whole hiring process over... all while balancing the store.

However, if one of your trusted employees recommends a great candidate for the company, you TRUST that person will only recommend a friend that would do a good job. The odds are better that their friends aren't complete weirdos so you'll be happy to offer them an interview.

I know this was just a job at Jamba Juice, but the side door is the number one approach to get any job.

Find a way to go through the side door.

The side door is any entrance other the front door, which includes:

- You knowing someone on the inside.

- Someone on the inside making an introduction to you and the recruiter.

- Your aunt's brother-in-law knows a friend of a cousin of a guy who she used to date that used to work at that company... and wants to introduce you.

Any connection, no matter how weak it is, will be stronger than no tie (unless it is a bad tie... which means don't have somebody that got fired from the company introduce you to the HR manager).

Pros:

- Easiest way to actually get hired.

- Gives recruiters a positive vibe about you before you even meet.

- Statistically the most effective way to land your internship

Cons:

- You have to know somebody (We will talk about networking soon, it is incredibly important)

Steven Rothberg, founder of CollegeRecruiter.com, says "[a]bout 90 percent of job openings go unadvertised, yet about 90 percent of candidates apply only to advertised job openings."

These jobs are being filled in by people who are going through the side door! Michael Ellsberg, author of *The Education of Millionaires*, emphasizes what is "*vastly more important, by orders of magnitude, is the strength of your network - the breadth and depth of the circle of people who trust you, feed you tips about job openings and would vouch for you to an employer as well as your demonstrable portfolio of real world skills.*"

How do you get in through the side door? Ask :)

My friend called me the other day and told me how passionate he was about project management, and asked if I could help him get a job at Intel. Fortunately for him, the friend I was grabbing dinner with at that moment was a Program Manager at Intel! I literally put him on hold and asked her if she could refer him, and she agreed.

The great thing for her is that companies actually pay their employees money if they successfully refer somebody, usually up to $5,000 or more. Why? Because recruiting GOOD TALENT is hard work and with this bonus incentive, everyone wins.

You never know who knows who, so it really doesn't hurt to put yourself out there and ask. And if you are afraid to ask your friend for help, you might have to evaluate two things:

1. Are they even your friend if you're afraid to ask them for help?

2. If you are too embarrassed to send a text to a friend, it doesn't seem like you want this internship badly enough.

The side door is the easiest door to get a job, but everyone prefers to go on Monster.com and spam 50+ resumes.

WHY!?

Because that's "easier" apparently. I don't know about you, but I like being productive, not busy.

How to Network

Your network is so, so, so much more important than what you have on your resume or what degree you have.

I wrote a book titled, *How To Network: Instantly Build Trust & Respect With Anyone You Meet*. In less than a week, it had over 2,000+ sales, 50+ reviews, and became an Amazon bestseller. Pretty rad for a first time author.

I would HIGHLY recommend you read *How To Network* because that book compliments job searching super well (it's a quick read).

No, this is not some sleazy sales pitch to buy more of my stuff. Email me and I'll send you a free PDF (writetotampham@gmail.com). Networking is so important, I'm willing to give up potential sales to help you succeed in your job search. But it's literally $3.99 on Amazon if you want to support, no pressure.

Regardless if you read it or not, I'll explain the cliff notes version here, just trust me that what I'm saying is true.

Networking = Making Friends

I used to think that to make "connections", you needed to shove business cards down people's faces, talk about golf, and be the most extroverted person in the room.

WRONG.

Friends are people who help you, support you, and appreciate you. Don't you want the same qualities from your "business connections" as well?

When you start to "network" with people, think of it as making friends. It's supposed to be fun.

GIVE, GIVE, GIVE. Then ask.

The most successful people are the ones who give the most frequently. As psychologist Robert Cialdini, the author of *Influence*, explains the law of reciprocity:

"The rule of reciprocity says that we should try to repay what another person has provided us. By virtue of the rule, we are obligated to the future repayment of favors, gifts, invitations, and the like.

When you consistently help other people, they will naturally come back to help you. Why does this work? Entrepreneur Gary Vaynerchuk sums it up beautifully,

"Because the truth is, people like people. We're wired for it. And people do business with other people. So when you learn to generally give to those people without expecting them to do something in return, you win. You'll perceive the world differently, and if we're being honest, be a better person because of it."

How do you give when you're just starting out and you've got nothing to give?

Michael Ellsberg interviewed networking expert Keith Ferrazzi about this question and he responded,

"The greatest gift you can give another person is the feeling of making a difference, a legacy, and importance.

The right way to go about it is to be generous with the person you want to connect with... tell a story. Tell a story about how you drew inspiration from their teachings and their example, how it impacted your life and all the ways you're passing that gift on to others now. If you move me enough with what you've accomplished with my teachings and how you're serving others, then yes, of course I want to help you!

I've helped all kinds of young people who have reached out to me with their stories of the amazing things they've done applying the concepts in my books. When I invest my time and effort in helping a young person, the dividend I receive in return is their gratitude, and their success."

What to give to others

On top of giving the feeling of importance, you can also give many things to help.

- Send them an article that they would enjoy reading based on their interests.

- Send them a book recommendation that you think they would really like.

- Send them an introduction to someone they HAVE to meet.

Silver Bullet

When it comes to giving, the most effective thing that you can give to somebody is IDEAS.

Most business leaders don't care about getting coffee with you. There's going to be five college students cold emailing an executive asking for coffee.

This business executive probably makes 6 figures a year and they don't need some teenager buying them coffee.

So why do students ALWAYS ASK PROFESSIONALS FOR COFFEE!?

You have to offer something of greater value. Money can work but it doesn't show that you have put any effort, time, and thought into your gift.

This is why IDEAS are the ultimate currency.

I've used this exact strategy to network with high-level speakers, entrepreneurs, and bestselling authors. Give ideas on how they can bring in more customers, increase their YouTube subscribers, or ideas to solve whatever they're focused on. Once you understand their needs with a genuine desire to help them, you can now form a much stronger relationship.

> *"You can have everything in life you want, if you will just help other people get what they want."*
>
> — *Zig Ziglar*

When it comes to going to the side door, you are going to have to establish a strong network, and there are a variety of ways to get started.

- Go to local events around your topic of interest. If you're interested in marketing, search for marketing meetups or conferences online.

- Join organizations related to your interests. This includes college clubs, professional fraternities, your local Rotary chapter, etc.

- Ask your existing network. You can literally post a Facebook status sharing your internship goals and ask for help. Tweet about it. Instagram a picture of yourself (#HireMe). I'm half kidding. But don't be afraid to put yourself out there.

- Ask your friends personally. Call them up, send them a text, or go to their house and simply share your story. You never know who knows who and how willing people are to help.

- Find online communities. There are different communities on sites like Facebook and LinkedIn that will help you meet cool people in your particular field.

- Cold message people on LinkedIn, Twitter, or any other network your new friends may be hanging out at!

With relationships, you have to think about the LONG GAME. Don't expect magic to happen overnight. Ferrazzi also shared how he put networking into action.

"When I was a kid, I built a relationship with the chairman of Baxter International at the time, Vernon Loucks. At least once a quarter, I would ping him, send him a simple update e-mail, and let him know how his advice was beneficial to me - how I applied it, how it's been helpful, then thank him effusively, praise how much I respect him, and then follow up right after that with another question. A quarter later, I'd tell him how I applied that advice, and what happened then. It was a lovely circle. I stayed in touch with him for years and years and years, it was a wonderful relationship."

What if I want to work at a specific company?

I spoke with John Salangsang who works as the Internship Specialist at San Jose State University and the first question he would ask the student is,

"Who do you know at that company?"

Student: "No one."

John: "That's going to have to change."

John would literally help that student find upcoming events (online and offline) to connect with people from that company. If you want to work at Google, for example, knowing someone on the inside will carry so much more weight than a stellar application.

I interviewed Andre Tacuyan on my podcast and he shared his journey on how he became an intern at Google. Tacuyan told me that since his friend's dad knew somebody at Google, he was able to put his name into the Google system under trusted referrals.

Because of this, Tacuyan had a flag next to his name so when the recruiters looked through the system, Tacuyan's application was instantly noticed.

Now the recruiter can skip hundreds of applications to read his flagged application first.

Tacuyan tells me this is common not just at Google, but at most companies. I don't know how much you can tell but networking is so important. You don't need to come from a rich family or have your dad work at some big-name company to get in through the side door. Anyone can build a world-class network.

With any new person you meet, make it a habit to always give, give, give first. Relationships take time to blossom and your job right now is to simply plant seeds.

Some might blossom faster than others. Don't force it. Don't rush anything. Don't be worried.

After you give, give, give to people you meet, make the ask. With the people you already know, it's okay to ask because you already have an established relationship. Invest in your network and benefits will come.

How does Networking ACTUALLY work in the real world?

Situation #1: Your friend works at the company

Say you want to work at Cisco (big tech company) and your friend Hung works there.

You can message Hung:

"Hey Hung!

Hope all is well :)

I'm looking to switch careers and I really want to work at Cisco. Do you mind if I ask you a few quick questions to see if I'll be a good fit?"

Since Hung is my friend, he'll be happy to help me. We can jump on the phone or meet in person since we're both local.

I'll share my story, how eager I am to learn and grow, and ask him for advice. If he knows somebody who has the power to hire me, he'll most likely offer an email introduction (before I even ask him for a job).

From there, I'll follow up with Hung to make sure he gets permission from HR for the introduction. (People HATE blind introductions, so make sure you get permission!)

Next, I'll type out the introduction draft and send it to Hung to save him time:

"Hi [Recruiter Name],

Hope all is well. As promised, I would love to introduce you to my friend Tam who would be a great fit for our marketing team. Attached is his personal website and resume if you're interested.

Tam,

[Recruiter Name] works as [Position Name] here at Cisco. [She/he] is [Interesting fact / Genuine Compliment about Recruiter]. I hope you two connect and help each other.

No need to cc me in future emails!

Best,

Hung"

Then you follow up immediately after Hung sends that email.

"Hey Hung,

Thanks so much for the kind introduction, I really appreciate it.

[Recruiter Name],

Nice to (virtually) meet you! Hung has told me nothing but great things about you and your work.

I would love to meet up and talk about how I can help Cisco. Would Tuesday or Wednesday afternoon of next week be a good time for you?

Best,

Tam"

Keep your emails short and sweet.

Wait for a reply and after a week of no response, follow up with the recruiter.

After two weeks of no response, follow up again. After three weeks of no response, you should ask Hung to check in and ask if anything is wrong with his friend.

Sometimes, recruiters are busy or bad with email.

Because Hung got their permission to connect you two, it's acceptable for him to reach out personally and give them a little reminder about the introduction.

But you might be wondering... What if Hung can't refer me directly? What if he just works in a specific department with no connection to the hiring team?

He'll help me see if I'm a good fit and give me insider advice on how to work at Cisco. I'll take detailed notes.

Then I'll ask him if he could connect me to anyone else at Cisco where I can learn more information. Since Hung works at Cisco, he mostly has co-workers he hangs out with who would be happy to help. If he says no, don't sweat it.

I'll then look at my notes, use his advice, and update him on my job search journey. I'll follow up two weeks later and share what has happened. I'll also try and find ways to give back to Hung, whether that's in the form of a small thank you present, a shout out on Twitter, or send him an article he might like.

Thanks Hung, you're the best!

Situation #2: Your friend knows somebody on the inside

Let's say I want to work for Cisco and my friend Kera knows Hung. The goal is to ask for an introduction from Kera to Hung. Before you ask, you must ask yourself: How well do you know Kera?

Because introductions are a special thing. I wouldn't want to introduce a random guy Jerry to my friend Kera if I knew Jerry was untrustworthy. Because if things don't go well with Jerry and Kera, guess who looks bad?

Me.

This is why people only give introductions to other people they love, trust, and respect. So how well do I know Kera? How much have I helped her? How does she perceive me?

Hopefully, you were never rude to her (or anyone else) and were always helpful. If you know Kera well enough, ask for the introduction.

"Hey Kera,

Hope all is well! I saw on LinkedIn that you know Hung who works at Cisco. I'm thinking about working at Cisco and I would love to ask him a few questions to see if I'll be a good fit. Can you connect us?

If yes, here is a permission email introduction you can use for your convenience.

'Hey Hung,

My good friend Tam is extremely curious about working at Cisco. Do you have 5 minutes for a quick phone call to see if he'll be a good fit?

Best,

Kera'

No pressure to say yes, will always be a friend. Keep up the great work, Kera :)

Best,

Tam"

BAM. Short and sweet. Plus, you have already done the heavy lifting for Kera so it's drop dead easy for her to copy and paste your email draft.

If she says no, don't sweat. Thank Kera and keep in touch. Find ways to give to Kera specifically just to make her life better, even when you might not get any benefits out of it. If she says yes, then jump back to Situation #1 and start that process all over again.

Situation #3 - You kind of know Kera but not well enough to ask for an introduction.

Like I mentioned, introductions are sacred. You don't want to introduce someone to your friend if that person isn't trustworthy. So how can you increase the trust between you and Kera?

Like I mentioned in my networking chapter, give, give, give and then ask for the introduction.

If you barely know Kera, you can also consider to give, give, give to Hung directly to simply save time.

Go ahead and message Hung directly and say something like,

"Hey Hung,

I'm a big fan of your work for [authentic reason].

I'm currently a student at [School] and your advice has helped me [accomplish THIS goal]. Just wanted to say thanks. Looking forward to keeping up with your journey through your [Website or Social Network]

Best,

Tam"

Notice how you didn't ask for anything. You simply admired his work and shared how much he has impacted your life! You have now planted a seed.

Depending on his response, you can engage in conversation and help in any way you can. THIS is how you build relationships: showing your appreciation by always offering to help. Always giving. NOT by asking.

Relationships require time. Don't expect Hung to "hook you up" with a job right away. Prove your worth. Provide value. Think about HIM before yourself.

If he sees your work and trusts you, then you can make that ask. Or he might even beat you to it and offer you the job because he saw your website in your email signature and you're that great.

What happens when the recruiter emails you back?

Ask for a time to chat either in person or over the phone.

What if they say no to connecting with you?

Thank them, and ask for advice on what your next steps should be. Find ways to give back to them. After two weeks, follow up with them and give an update on how you used their advice to get results!

If you are serious about keeping a relationship with the recruiter, find ways to give and send updates on your journey.

Emailing Recruiters

One time, I needed to sell tickets to a rave. I posted a Facebook status about it and my friend commented, "Hey Tam! My friend's cousin's brother-in-law wants to buy it!"

The "normal person" would message that friend and play the waiting game.

"Hey! You wanted to buy the ticket?"

"How much are you selling it for?"

"$100⊠

"Okay, let me go and contact my friend's cousin who will contact her brother-in-law and see."

You wait two days.

"Hey Tam, how many do you have?"

"I have 2.⊠

"Okay, let me tell them."

Zzzzzzz.

THIS WILL TAKE DAYS AND YOU WILL NEVER SELL YOUR TICKET!

Solution? Avoid the middleman and go straight to the source.

I'll say something to my friend like,

"Hey! I hate to bother you and your friend's cousin as middlemen because this shouldn't be your responsibility. May I talk to your friend's cousin's brother-in-law directly? Things would be much easier and would relieve stress for both you and your cousin.

If you like the idea, may I please have his phone number? Or if he prefers, here is my phone number so that he can contact me.

What do you think?"

"Oh of course Tam! That would be much better actually. Let me look up his number for you right now."

Okay, enough about raves.

You can find the HR manager at the company you want to work for and cold email them directly. There are two different types of emails you can send: Referral and Direct.

Referral Email Template

Subject: Can you point me in the right direction?

Hi [Name],

I noticed your opening intern position on [source] and I wanted to ask, are you still hiring for that position? If so, who should I contact? If it makes it easier, my resume is attached if you simply want to forward it over (less work on you!).

Looking forward to hearing from you.

Thanks,

Tam

Direct Email Template

Subject: [Referral] told me to reach out to you! :)

Hi [Name],

[Referral] told me that you were the best person to talk to about the [Internship Position]. Is the position still open? I'm a student at [School] eager to immerse myself into [Field of Study] and I'm confident that I will bring a ton of value to help [Company].

Looking forward to hearing from you.

Thanks,

Tam

In both of the emails, I was polite and did not come off desperate. The goal is to get a reply back, not to land the job on the spot.

Note: These are my own basic email scripts. You can edit and personalize them as much as you want. I just want to give you a starting point.

Will going through the side door require more work? Yes.

Will this be more effective? Hell yes.

Pro tip: TRACK YOUR EMAILS (for cold emails) so you don't have to keep on checking back frantically. I recommend YesWare.com or BoomerangGmail. com. You can see when they opened it and then you can follow up after a week of non-response.

This is how you network to get a job.

Job Fairs

A job fair, also commonly referred to as a career fair or career expo, is a place for employers, recruiters, and schools to meet with prospective job seekers.

If you see a bunch of tables or booths giving away company swag, you're probably at the right place. If you do go through this side door, let's go through how to ROCK IT at your next job fair.

a) Research, research, research!

The number one complaint employers have at job fairs is that the students have no idea what the company does when they first meet them.

The recruiters are there to find the best talent and aren't thrilled to give another elevator pitch on what they do.

Research all the companies you're interested in depth BEFORE you actually speak with them. Instead of just learning about what they do, you are coming into the conversation ready with how you will be a great fit for their team.

b) Research job descriptions

Some job fairs even post job descriptions of the positions they're looking to hire so ask whoever is hosting the job fair for that information.

Why?

You can then tailor your resume (ahead of time) and know the exact words to convey how you relate to their company's job description.

c) Come as early as possible

Throughout the whole day, the recruiter is going to talk to HUNDREDS of students. They're not going to remember everyone.

This is your chance to make a great first impression when they're fresh and ready to go. Some job fairs may have an Early Bird Pass which gets you access to the job fair before everyone else. Find out if there are any hidden perks you can upgrade to.

d) Dress like you're going into an interview (Covered in next chapter)

"Dress for the job you want, not the one you have."

Also, please leave your backpack at home. You'll look ten times better without it.

e) Have an "elevator pitch"

Imagine if you meet a recruiter in an elevator and you have 15 seconds to say who you are before they go to the next floor.

What are you going to say?

Since job fairs are so crowded with students, you have to make a strong first impression right at the get go.

I don't really like "an elevator pitch" because I hate the structure and the "un-humanness" of it, but if you're new to this game, it is a great starting point.

An elevator pitch is a very quick overview about whatever you're pitching (in this case, you) so that the other person quickly understands the concept (your experience and unique story).

At the basic level, you can say something like:

Hi, My name is [Name]. I will be graduating from [University] with a degree in [Field of Study] I came across your [Company] and I loved [Authentic Reason]. I have some ideas that I could help solve [Company Problem]. May I tell you about them?

If you have researched the company and have ideas on how you can benefit beforehand, you are so ahead of the game. By having ideas specifically, the recruiter can instantly can tell that you've done your homework and they will remember you for that.

One last tip:

f) Do. Not. Be. A. Robot.

Staffing Agency

Another side door you can use is through a staffing agency. Staffing agencies help you get hired for a company that works with them.

Seems too good to be true?

Pros:

- They do the heavy lifting. All you have to do is worry about the interview (mostly).

- They can open doors that maybe you, your friends, or your school can't.

Cons:

- The search is out of your control. Who knows where it will go?

- Limited opportunities

Research the validity and success rate with any staffing agency you want to use. Like anything in life, some are great, and some aren't so great.

Professors

If you're in college, your professors are the most underrated resource for introductions. If you're in their class and you're a diligent and hardworking student, they'll be more than happy to help you on your job search.

I've had friends received job offers simply because the professor connected that student to a recruiter (usually their old friend) over email. There are other instances where the professor invites the student to intern directly under them, making that a unique and awesome opportunity.

You never know until you ask!

Portfolio companies

These are companies that allow you to create a super detailed profile on their platforms, and they have employers actually call you! I don't have much experience using these platforms but I know of one reputable source that I would love to share.

AfterCollege.com

AfterCollege has been around for 15+ years and reaches over five million students. They are the real deal (no, they're not paying me to say this. I wish they were though).

In short, there are so many potential side door options that you can choose. Your existing network is your most effective option because of the strong relationships you already have. Never discount the potential from your friends.

Put yourself out there. Go to events. Meet new people. Give, give, give. Then ask. Work with what you got. You got this. :)

CREATIVE APPROACH

~

This is one of my favorite approaches because of how easily it makes you stand out from the crowd.

The creative approach to job searching is not going through the front door but taking an out of the box approach to get noticed.

Paiman Vahdati

Paiman Vahdati was a normal guy who really wanted a Creative Marketing position at Indiegogo, a crowd funding website, except there were a few problems.

1. The Creative Marketing position didn't exist.

2. The staff wasn't hiring. As in, there were no open positions on the website or on any job sites.

3. Paiman didn't know anyone who worked at Indiegogo.

Despite all of this, Vahdati was able to get an interview with the Head of Marketing at Indiegogo just a few weeks later. How?

I interviewed Vahdati on my podcast and tried to deconstruct what was going on in his mind doing this creative approach. Vahdati emphasized that to get what you want, you have to go above and beyond the expectations. In his own words:

"Think about what an average person would do. And do the opposite."

Starting his creative job approach, Vahdati made sure to identify his dream company to work for and at that time, it was Indiegogo.

The next step was to find out what problems Indiegogo had. How could Vahdati use his skills and talents to help the company? He felt like marketing the platform to new users would really help the company and that was what he focused on.

Next, he had to show off his skills and experiences. Vahdati knew a standard resume wouldn't do it, so he did something better. Vahdati created an Indiegogo campaign for HIMSELF.

For raising money, he replaced the $$$ goal with how many hours he was willing to work. Under perks and special rewards, he wrote all of his skills, projects, and awards. In the body description, he wrote about his experiences and the value he could bring to Indiegogo. In the video portion of the page (front and center), he created a picture showing off his greatest accomplishments establishing his credibility. And if you look at the campaign, the design is absolutely beautiful. Vahdati told me it took him over 10 hours to complete it and I asked him the obvious question:

What if you don't get the position? Wouldn't everything just be a waste?

"It wouldn't be a waste at all. Regardless if I got it or not, I would have learned a ton of things. I worked my design, outreach, and my creativity skills. Even if this application didn't go 'viral,' I'm on this podcast aren't I?"

The next question was, where are the decision makers of Indiegogo hanging out at? Vahdati did his research and found that most of the executive team were active on Twitter, LinkedIn, and email.

He tweeted the team. Vahdati asked his friends to favorite and retweet the tweets. Vahdati reached out on LinkedIn and through email. It got to the point where Vahdati's friend even forwarded his creative resume to the CEO of Indiegogo!

Vahdati wasn't sure which specific action moved the needle but a few weeks later, Paiman received a note asking what time they should set up the interview.

BAM.

And that was Vahdati's goal. To get his foot in the door and get the interview. After that, Vahdati was on his own.

During the interview, Vahdati created and sent a 30-60-90 plan exclusively for Indiegogo. This plan outlined what he wanted to help accomplish in the first 30 days, the 30 days after that, and the 30 days after that.

"This proves that you're not all talk. You don't need someone to hold your hand. Having a 30-60-90 plan [or any kind of ideas] shows that you are ambitious and serious about making a contribution to the organization."

Unfortunately, there was literally no opening at that specific time. They were planning to expand the team in Q4, which was a month from that phone call.

I asked Vahdati if that journey was a failure then, and he said not at all.

"This is my foot in the door. When the marketing position opens up, I'm already in contact with the Head of Marketing. And while everyone else is applying online, I'll already be 10 steps ahead of the game."

Another stellar example features Nina Mufleh creating a website (http://www.nina4airbnb.com) specifically for Airbnb showcasing who she is, what her experience was, and her passion for the company.

One of the best things that she did was give the Airbnb team concrete ideas on what she could immediately work on if she was hired. The designed mirrored Airbnb's website, and all of her website copy was tailored specifically for a job function that wasn't even open.

Her website went viral, getting covered in multiple publications gathering millions of hits. This of course got Brian Chesky's, the CEO of Airbnb, attention.

Nina received an interview, and although Airbnb did not hire her, she received dozens of job offers from other notable companies because of her creativity.

It was amazing to witness.

WHICH PATH SHOULD YOU TAKE?

Work backwards from your goal.

If your goal was to become a marketing intern for a local company, which avenues would have the greatest impact? I would assume my top three options would be:

1. Side Door (Should usually be first)

2. University's Career Center

3. Job Fairs

If your goal was to work for a startup, which avenues might have the greatest impact?

1. Side Door

2. Creative Approach

3. Emailing Recruiters (or in many cases, the founders!)

If your goal was to work for Google, which avenues might have the greatest impact?

1. Side Door

2. Staffing Agency

3. Emailing Recruiters

These avenues are all assumptions because each person has different career goals and objectives. Other avenues may be better for you in regards to your unique situation.

Choose one avenue, spend 30 minutes every day, and see what results you will have. After every job application, you should send a follow up email after a week of not hearing back. If a week has flown by and you haven't seen any results, you can ask yourself a few questions:

1. Is this the right avenue for me and my situation?

2. Is my story not clear on my resume and cover letter?

3. Did a technical error happen and my application didn't go through?

The reason we are not doing all of the channels at once is because we want to be efficient and effective. The point is to not have your hands in too many cookie jars because you lose focus. Literally, you can lose focus and forget what jobs you applied for.

Which brings up a good point: Keep track of all the jobs you applied for!

A basic spreadsheet works.

Remember, follow up with each company after a week if you don't hear a response. Don't think that you're not "good enough" if they don't get back to you. It's normal. Sometimes, the recruiters have too much work on their plate. The position might have already been filled, or the recruiter might be having a bad day.

AFU: Always Follow Up.

So Tam, how would you try to get a job at Google if you had no network?

The first question I would ask myself is, am I even qualified to work at Google? What value can I bring to make Google even want me?

If I'm a freshman in college with no work experience, applying to Google might be unrealistic. Even if I had a strong network, chances are slim because I literally have proven nothing and I have no value to give.

That's like a homeless guy trying to date an attractive and successful woman; it's just not going to happen.

For this example, let's say I had the strong technical skills. Next I would ask myself: Do I even want to work at Google? I would then proceed to have different informational interviews to understand if Google would be a good fit for me and my career goals.

For this example, let's just say Google is indeed a good fit. The next question I would ask is: Who do I know at Google? I'll know the five people I did an informational interview with and use their advice on how to get my foot in the door. After I meet them, I should have already understood how the application process works. I would have also done my research online looking at different communities, reading blogs, and following Google news.

I would find out that to apply for their summer internships, there is an online application (front door) which usually opens in October. I would look and research the questions to make sure I understand everything.

I would then answer all the questions on a separate Word document. Next, I would try to meet people who work at Google or know people who work at Google (side door). I would find upcoming events in my area that Googlers might go to. I will also find online communities what Googlers participate in or people who know Googlers.

I'll go on LinkedIn.com, directly find people who work at Google, and cold message them. As I'm cultivating these relationships online and offline by giving, giving, and giving... I'm also tailoring my website for Google (creative approach).

Depending on the position I'm applying for, I'll transform my website to make it specific to that position. If I were to apply for a design position, I would showcase my website with my portfolio and write in specifically why I want to work at Google.

Within one week, I would probably make at least 10 connections to Googlers, understand the application process, and create an awesome website just for Google.

If I keep this up for one month, who knows how likely it is that I'll get an interview? Or if my application will get noticed. I'm using a combination of the front door, side door, and the creative approach!

Does this take more work? Yeah.

Would it be worth it? Hell yeah.

I could spend the next few years at Google building my skills and network all because I spent a few extra hours on my job application. Sacrificing some time now for a better life and career is a no-brainer.

Key Takeaways:

- Go through the side door whenever you can.

- Be knowledgeable of all the different ways to land internships. Each avenue has its pros and cons. Choose the one that is most relevant to your situation.

- Keep track of all the jobs you apply for and all the people you meet. Give, give, and give!

Action Steps:

- Create a spreadsheet

- Choose your top three avenues

- Now choose your top avenue and start your job search

- Keep track of every company you applied to on the spreadsheet and the date you sent in the application

- Follow up with non-responders after one week

- Reflect on your efforts. What is working well? What is not working well? Can you focus more energy and time into the avenues that work?

- Make improvements to your job search. That could mean improving your resume even more, switching channels from front door to side door, or even going to more events.

- Continue to make relationships with people in your desired space.

- Make all of this a habit and spend 30+ minutes working on your job search every day. This takes work, don't give up.

PART FOUR

INTERVIEW PREPARATION

Think about the house you're in right now. When do you think a house is built? If you think it's during construction, guess again. Houses are built in the drawing room, before a brick ever touches another brick.

Bigger Picture: Before your interview, you have to immensely prepare.

Before you say a word in your interview, the recruiter will instantly know if you have done your homework and practiced. My philosophy? Similar to the rest of the book, do all of the work upfront so that when you go into the interview, you've already won.

What do you need to do before your interview?

1) Do your research.

"One of the biggest complaints of hiring managers is that many job interview candidates know very little about the company they're interviewing for."

- Andy Teach, author of *From Graduation to Corporation: The Practical Guide to Climbing the Corporate Ladder One Rung at a Time*

Here are the very basic things you should ask yourself:

- How much do you know about what the company does?

- How much do you know about their products or services?

- Where is the company today and where do you think they should be three months from now? Six months? 12 months?

- What are some of the company's biggest problems that you can help improve or solve?

- Who is interviewing you, and what is that person's background or experience in?

30 minutes of scanning their website is not enough research. Dive deeper into their business and be confident you know their company inside and out.

2) Remember that no one cares about you.

You read that correctly.

NO ONE CARES ABOUT YOU. ALL THEY CARE ABOUT IS THEMSELVES.

Are you mad at me? Sorry, I can be a real douche.

But in all seriousness, the recruiters have a job to do. They need to hire great talent to positively help the company. So recruiters are thinking about:

- Are YOU going to make them look bad?

- Are YOU going to commit to your job?

- Are YOU going to be a good team player?

- Are YOU going to exceed at your position?

- Are YOU going to be the right fit for the company?

This mentality isn't evil, it's just business. But now that we know the rules, let's learn how to win the game.

The main principle behind interviewing is that your answers should show how you can provide massive amounts of value to them. We'll dive into more specific tactics later in the chapter.

3) "Would I be down to have a beer with this intern after work?"

Have you ever had an interview where you went in talking about school and what you're studying... and end the interview talking about how the Golden State Warriors are doing? Although not every interview will end with sports, the majority of my interviews end with both of us laughing at something completely irrelevant to the job.

How do I do this?

I'm no angel that fell out of the sky (or so I think) but there are tactics to build this rapport.

Biggest lesson I've learned? Make the interview a conversation.

Let's think back: What do employers want?

They don't JUST want an intern to do the work. Anyone can do work. They want to bring someone that they trust. Employers care about your accomplishments and skills but if they get the vibe that you are not fun to work with, THEY WILL NOT HIRE YOU.

End of story.

Get into the mindset of connecting with them on a personal level and earning their trust. At the end of the day, they're going to ask themselves,

"Would I be down to have a beer with this intern after work?"

4) Questions and Answers

Before we dive in, let's talk about the best way to study Q&A's by debunking some myths.

- Do NOT have scripted answers to all of the possible interview questions.

There are hundreds of possible interview questions. DON'T WORRY ABOUT ALL OF THEM.

"But Tam... what if they ask me a question I'm not prepared for?"

You don't need to be prepared for every single answer. As long as you have the key principles in set, you'll be able to answer any question in an intelligent fashion. In short, memorization and scripted answers for every single question is the recipe for stress and failure.

- Do NOT practice with your family members.

Unless your family members are skilled interviewers or professionals in that space, don't practice with them. They're biased, and you may even get frustrated.

Instead, practice interviewing with TRUSTED friends, teachers, professors, professionals, or even people that you have done your informational interviews with. They can give you honest and genuine feedback on your body language, tone of voice, answer choices, etc.

- Do NOT read your answers out loud repetitively to practice memorization.

When you "practice" interviewing, ACTUALLY TALK AS IF YOU WERE IN THE INTERVIEW. Reading your typed answers is NOT the same as practicing. Go find somebody and actually talk to them as if they were the interviewer.

Which is better: Playing tennis against a wall or playing tennis against someone who is better than you? When you play with another human, you practice "in-game" hits. When you play against the wall, you practice hits that you won't actually use in a real game. Practice your "in-game" interview questions.

- Do NOT practice in front of a mirror

When you speak in front of a mirror, how can you concentrate on both your answers and your facial expressions?

Instead, you should record yourself. Yes, it'll be slightly uncomfortable, but you can clearly see how you come across while answering interview questions.

5) The Actual Questions and Answers

Imagine you are writing an autobiography about yourself. You can start rambling about your life and everything you've done since you were two years old, but the strategic thing to do is pick a handful of experiences you want to highlight and paint a concise story.

To start acing interviews, write down five focus points in your life that you want to highlight about yourself.

It could be your past work experience, club activities at your school, volunteer work. Whatever is most relevant to the job position you're applying for.

Let's use my friend Bobby as an example. Here are his five focus points:

1. Outreach Coordinator for Alpha Kappa Psi

2. Barista at Starbucks

3. Sales Internship at Greenpeace

4. Volunteer at Red Cross Hospital

5. Member of Entrepreneurship Club

When you answer any interview question, make sure you are always talking about the BENEFIT you will have for the company. You can conquer any interview question if you understand your focus points and be in the mindset of helping the company.

Bobby is applying for a business internship and they ask him:

1) What have you done at your previous job positions?

*Bobby: I did a **sales internship at GreenPeace** where I had to persuade people to donate to our organization in hopes to fund our global initiatives. I honestly started off slow but after getting over my fear of rejection, I increase my sales to 15 a week and became the top salesperson in our division. With my leadership and business experience, I'm really excited to see how I can properly apply my skills to your current and future projects.*

2) Describe a challenge you had to face and how you got over it.

Bobby: A challenge I had at my first job really tested my limits.

*It was my second month as a **barista at Starbucks** when all hell broke loose. It was a hot summer day, and the line was out the door and around the corner. We were short on inventory, including many of the different syrups needed to make our classic drinks, and it didn't help to also be short staffed.*

Everyone in line started to get frustrated and impatient. I don't know what came over me but I stepped out to the front of the store, stood in front of the customers and said,

"Hey everyone, thanks for being here at Starbucks. We're currently short staffed and missing some inventory which is why the line is moving slower than usual. We are doing the best we can to get the drinks made as fast as possible and I just wanted to let you know our situation. There are many different Starbucks out there and we appreciate you coming into our lovely store. You'll get your drinks shortly. Thanks so much for your patience."

Applause broke out as I walked back behind the counter. Impatient customers started to smile. My manager looked at me with his jaw wide open and I grinned back at her.

When I see any problems with the team or customers, I am not afraid to access the situation and resolve the conflict accordingly.

3) Why should we hire you?

*Bobby: On your job description, you mentioned you wanted someone who is motivated, ambitious, and a creative thinker. With my passion for marketing and my experience working for **GreenPeace, Starbucks, and Alpha Kappa Psi**, it's a no-brainer to join forces with you and add to your ongoing success.*

I understand you only want to hire people who believe in your mission and I truly admire how you go out of your way to have a social impact within the community.

4) What extracurricular activities do you do ?

*Bobby: On top of my Fraternity work, I'm an active **volunteer at the Red Cross Hospital** and also a member of my **Entrepreneurship Club**. I joined Red Cross because I have worked with them throughout high school and was able to meet some really awesome people while doing meaningful work.*

Because my teachers have always complimented me as being ambitious, they convinced me to join the Entrepreneurship Club where I also met many like-minded thinkers. Next week, I'm entering a business plan competition with members from the club so that's going to be fun.

With all of these different experiences, I'm able to learn valuable lessons and apply these skills back to helping your company.

What do you notice from these interview questions?

Bobby is telling stories on his experience or as we called it, focus points. You can tell someone that you handle conflict well, but when you share a story on how you expertly handled an angry line of customers, that is when you will win.

You can also tell that Bobby has done his homework. Bobby mentions the exact wording on the company's job description that matches his strengths and abilities. Bobby also mentioned specific details like how he knew the social impact the company makes to their community, and how excited he was to be a part of that.

Instead of studying a million different interview questions, you already have a core foundation on what you want to say, which can be integrated into most interview questions.

This method is the definition of working smarter, not harder.

It's easier said than done, like most things in life, but it works. And I'm surprised students are still "memorizing" scripts. because. robotic. answers. will. not. get. the. interviewer. to. trust. or. like. them. lol.

Once you have these your key focus points, you can practice intensely with those stories first. Feel free to add more experiences to your arsenal but having five experiences gives you a starting point on the bigger picture of how to conquer an interview.

Last but not least, to really impress the interviewer, I recommend you to...

COME UP WITH IDEAS ON HOW TO HELP THEM!

When the interviewer is finished with Bobby's interview and they ask,

"Is there anything you want to ask me?"

Now is his chance to impress them even more with IDEAS.

Bobby: I noticed that you were struggling to gain more Twitter followers for your company account. From my research, it seems that a lot of your tweets aren't being optimized for maximum engagement. I brought a print out of sample tweets that I wrote for you to test out if you were interested, along with the best times to schedule the posts for maximum engagement.

[Pull out paper with pre-written tweets and images]

Because of my experience on my own Twitter account and work for my fraternity, I have found massive success with engagement if you make a few small tweaks.

When the interviewer sees you have already studied their Twitter account and done work to help them, they will be absolutely surprised. This is the absolute WOW factor, and these ideas don't have to be with just Twitter.

Find a problem that the company may be facing (preferably a problem that you can solve with your intern position) and write ideas on how you can improve on it.

- Write 10 ideas on how they can sell more products

- Write 10 ideas on where they should focus their marketing efforts

- Write 10 ideas on how they can improve their social media presence

- Write 10 ideas on which organizations they can potentially partner with

- Write 10 ideas on what events they can collaborate on to increase their exposure

Ideas work MARVELOUSLY. When you show them GOOD IDEAS, they will be blown away by the extra effort you've done. We want to work smarter, not harder, so congrats. You've done your homework.

Key Takeaways:

- You win the interview before the interview
- Research the company in depth
- No one really cares about you
- Make the interview a conversation
- Focus points > Memorized answers
- Generate ideas and help solve the company's problems

Action:

- Research everything you can about the company. Aim for a minimum of one hour a day for seven days.
- Write five experiences and practice crafting your stories.
- Practice with trusted people and receive honest and genuine feedback.
- Find the company's problems and generate ten ideas to help.

PHONE OR SKYPE INTERVIEWS

If it is a phone or Skype interview, here are a few things you should be prepared for before speaking:

1. Distraction free zone: Remove all papers, books, food, or anything that might distract you from the interview.

2. Quiet environment: The worst thing you can do is be at a noisy Starbucks yelling into the phone. Pick a quiet place in your house or your backyard to do your interview at.

3. Glass of water: Keep fluids in your body at all time. Water also calms your nerves.

4. Use the restroom beforehand: Speaking of nerves, don't forget to pee!

5. Have focus points in front of you: Don't have an immediate answer to the question? No sweat! You have your stories in front of you that you can use at any time.

6. Have your resume in front of you: Since you sent them your resume, they'll most likely be referring to it throughout the interview. Have yours out as well so that you can follow along.

7. Have your ideas ready: Remember how important ideas were? This

is your chance to literally show them that you've done MORE than your homework on the company.

8. Smile: Since it's not in person, the human connection is harder to achieve but when you smile and talk as if the interviewer was in front of you, that connection will be stronger!

9. Dress for success: If it's a Skype interview, dress up! Treat it seriously.

10. Kill it.

In Person Interview

For an in-person interview, have these items prepared:

1) Bring 8 copies of your resume

Why 8? I don't know. But at least 5. I had a surprise group interview once and luckily I had enough resumes for everyone in the room.

2) Clean outfit

Let's talk about fashion, because I am obviously qualified. Prepare your outfit a few night before so you have it ready to go. Research the company you're interviewing with and see what their dress code is. For most interviews, both genders should stick to formal attire.

But if you're interviewing with a startup, do more research if a casual shirt and jeans would be more appropriate.

3) Directions

Get a few things clear before leaving your house:

- Make sure you know the exact address

- Research how traffic will be at that time

- Know exactly what parking lot you'll be at

- Find out what building you should enter through

- Double check if you have the room information correct

If being prepared means going up a day before to survey the land, DO IT. I once was late to an interview by 15 minutes because there was a huge traffic jam, and since the company had three different parking lots with all the buildings spaced out, the interview room was super hard to find.

Not a pleasant experience.

4) Contact Information

Always have their contact information saved on your phone.

If an emergency happens and you know you're going to be late, you don't have to... dig through your phone, look at the email thread, copy the number, call the wrong number, check back at your email, keep searching, then finally call them with your frantic and panicked voice all while driving to find a parking spot (true story for me).

5) Ideas

The reason I'm bringing this up again because it's so important: NO ONE WILL HAVE IDEAS FOR THEM BUT YOU WILL. Be special and helpful.

"Just.... DOOOOOOOO IIITTTTTT!!!!!!"

—*Shia LaBeouf*

BEFORE THE INTERVIEW

a) Make sure you get a good night's rest

If your sleeping schedule is messed up, you have to start sleeping well *at least a week in advance.*

Meaning that if you have an interview Monday morning, don't stay up Saturday night until 4am, sleep on Sunday night at 9pm, and expect to wake up alert the next day. Your body is like an internal clock and your sleep patterns need to stay consistent.

If you plan to sleep at 9pm the night before your interview, plan ahead! Starting from the Monday of last week, sleep at 9pm to get your body used to a regular sleeping schedule. That means skipping a party or two. It's not the end of the world.

b) Exercise on the morning of

Your body and mind are much more awake after you exercise. It will help you be alert for the interview.

c) Eat a good breakfast

Food energizes the brain. Eat a healthy breakfast with plenty of fruits and liquids!

d) Do NOT practice your Q&A answers

It's too late. Practicing on the day of is like cramming for a final. You're destined to fail because you're only going to memorize the stuff you're cramming in.

Just relax.

If you've already been practicing for the last few weeks, you have already prepared.

e) Watch standup comedy

I got this advice from bestselling author James Altucher and it actually works! I watch standup comedy before speeches, dates, and meetings because it puts you in a relaxed and happy state of mind.

You also observe their strong body language. Stand up comics deal with so much pressure and fear but they are some of the most confident speakers because of it.

Learn from them and have a good laugh.

f) Relax your mind

- Read books

- Write something

- Meditate (for beginners, I would recommend the app, Headspace)

The point of all this is to relax your mind. Don't be stressed out trying to cram an essay beforehand, getting into a fight with your significant other, or anything else.

Focus on the interview by not focusing on the interview.

g) Forget all the body language tips you know

You hear all these tips like, "Act confident by having a straight back" or "Increase your dominance by puffing your chest up." Or some fluffy advice like that.

I'm going to tell you a fact.

No matter how many body language tips you memorize, it will not matter unless your SUBCONSCIOUS is in the right state.

What are you talking about Tam?

It is *impossible* to consciously control all of your body language because you can't broadcast "confident" body language at will if your mind doesn't believe it. If your mind is nervous, your body will be nervous. If your mind is scared, your body will act scared.

You have to internally create a state of confidence or charisma.

Sure, you can study these body language cues. Fake it till you make it. Whatever. It'll work but not for long.

The best way is to get your head in the right place.

"Where your mind believes, your body manifests."

Truly believe that you will ace this interview. Tell yourself ten times out loud if you need to. You've put in the work. You've done your research. You've practiced every single day.

You've got this.

Key Takeaways:

- Be prepared for your interview
- Get your mind in the right state
- Do not cram or try to rush anything in

Actions:

- Pack eight copies of your resume
- Plan your entire outfit
- Plan what you will eat for breakfast
- Plan your workout time in the morning
- Get a good night's sleep starting from the week before your interview
- Plan what you will do before you interview (reading? standup comedy?)
- Have directions and interviewer's contact info ready
- Have your ideas ready and memorize
- Kill it!

OWN THE INTERVIEW

You found clarity on the jobs you wanted, completed your resume and cover letter, prepared for your interview and now you're finally here. Great job, you have already done all of the hard work.

If you've prepared well, this is the easiest part. It's like performing your high school play. If you practiced every day and memorized all of your lines, the performance should be a piece of cake since you've done it so many times.

Let's dive in.

The interview starts when you park. Here is a life lesson for everything in life: People are ALWAYS watching you. Even when you don't see anyone. Be on your absolute best behavior.

1) Get there early

How early? At least 30 minutes early. I don't care if anyone tells you that it is a waste of time. Wait in the car if you have to and go in at the 18 minute mark (it usually takes me three minutes to walk into the building from the parking lot) so that you arrive in the office precisely 15 minutes early.

2) Say hi to the receptionist

When you walk in and talk to the receptionist, make her smile. Seriously.

She'll say something like, *"Hi, good morning!"* Instead of responding, *"I have a 9am interview..."* Say,

"Hey Christine (Look at her name badge). Good morning to you, too! It's great to be here. How are you doing?"

The point is to engage in conversation before she asks you why you're here. Compliment her (for an authentic reason) and simply talk to her.

Connecting instantly with the receptionist is key. Because who is the hiring manager going to talk to right after they walk you out of the office? Talking also helps you become more confident by speaking comfortably and relieving the nerves you might have.

3) Don't use your phone

I know we live in the 21st century and there are Snapchats we "have" to check, but avoid your phone.

EVERYONE IS WATCHING YOU. Potential co-workers. Guests. Even the receptionist.

Although you are not harming anyone for using your phone, you *can* be doing something better. You want to look patient and be grateful that you're here. Here are some things that I personally do:

- I survey the room and read the awards they have on the wall

- I look at the flyers on the desk

- I glaze over the room

- I look over my resume one last time

- I drink some water

- I talk to the receptionist again (if it is appropriate)

- I breathe. Four long counts inhale, four counts hold, four counts exhale. This helps relieve your nerves.

- I don't check my phone. Snapchat can wait.

4) First impression

When you see the hiring manager, give a nice firm handshake and look them in the eyes. Smile. :)

Remember, you are going to OWN this interview! You have already done all the hard work. No need to be nervous. Answer the questions just like you have been practicing. Don't think of it as a question and answer discussion, but as a genuine conversation.

5) Thank them

As you leave, thank them for the interview and the opportunity. SUPER PRO TIP: SAY BYE TO THE RECEPTIONIST, and use her first name.

"Bye Christine! Have a good day!"

Bonus points if you can call back something you were talking about. For example, if you were chatting about the Warriors, you can say something like...

"Bye Christine, it was great to meet you. Hopefully Stephen Curry scores 30 points tonight..."

Or something like that. Call back something that you two were talking about. This is a tactic used frequently in comedy and it is SUPER effective because it proves that you were actually listening.

6) Make it to your car

Your interview ends when you leave their parking lot. Remember, people are always watching. Walk out confidently and always be on your best behavior.

Congrats! Your hard work is about to pay off.

Key Takeaways:

- People are always watching you
- Your interview starts when you park and ends when you drive off
- Always be on your best behavior
- Make a strong first impression
- Say thank you

Action:

- Read the next chapter

AFTER THE INTERVIEW

~

So you have done your research, practiced your butt off, and aced your interview. Congrats! Most people don't EVER make it to this level so give yourself a pat on the back.

What's next?

No matter how good your interview was, you have to follow up with the person you interviewed with to thank them for their time.

If the company is more old fashioned, consider keeping your message formal. If the employer is a small startup, write your message that mirrors their website copy and messaging.

It all depends on the context.

If you send a message to me, I don't really care if you're informal. But to the Google executive, an informal message may come off as immature.

You can say "thank you" in a variety of ways:

a) Handwritten Letter:

In a world where snail mail is ignored, a handwritten thank you card mailed to their office will definitely stand out. I highly recommend this option.

What should you write in your thank you card?

Dear [Interviewer #1] ,

Thanks for a great conversation about [what you talked about] last [day of the week]. I really enjoyed talking about [call back something you talked about] with you.

I look forward to continuing our discussion and seeing how I can help [Company Name] when I hear back from you.

Sincerely,

[Name]

How many cards should you send?

Send a personalized card to every person you interviewed with. If three different people interviewed you, send each of them three different cards.

b) Email

You could send an email but since we live in such a digital age, it won't come off as thoughtful or sincere as a handwritten letter. But if you want to stick with email, here is a sample template from www.job-hunt.org that you can use.

Subject: Thank you for the *[Job Title]* position interview on *[date]*

Dear *[Mr./Ms. Last Name]*:

Thank you very much for your time today *[or yesterday or the date]* to interview me for the position of *[job title]*. I appreciate the opportunity to learn more about this job, to meet you and *[names of other interviewers]*, and to see your facility *[or offices, location, whatever is appropriate]*.

[Reference anything you said that seemed important to the interviewer, like: As we discussed, I find the technology related to using cloud computing fascinating and an amazing opportunity for the future, but security is also a major concern. Keeping XYZ Company's information safe would be a top priority for the person in this job, and I would love to dig deeply into the protective technologies, as well as the threats, to avoid future problems.]

[Reference the "connection" you may have made, like: I enjoyed finding someone else who attended XYZ College and also roots for the hockey team. Hope they make the NCAA Division finals next year!]

As we discussed, I have *[months or years]* of experience with *[technology, tools, or qualification you have that seemed most important in the interview]*. With my background and experience, I believe that I could become a contributor to your team very quickly.

I am excited about this opportunity to join *[organization name]*. Please do not hesitate to email or call me if you have any questions or need any additional information.

I look forward to hearing from you *[whenever they said they would be in touch or in 10 days if they didn't give you a date]*.

Best regards,

[Your name]

[Your job title or tagline, like "eCommerce Customer Support Specialist"]

[LinkedIn Profile URL]

*[Phone number -- **not** your work number if you are employed]*

When should you follow up if they don't respond?

I'd recommend following up through email after two weeks of no response. Politely remind them that you're super excited for the position and are wondering when you can expect to hear back from them.

GLORY

~⁀

Say you went on seven different interviews and you received three offers on the table. Congrats! WHOOOOO!!!

Call your parents. Tell your friends. Go get some Taco Bell.

Once you're settled down, you have a decision to make. Which company should you work for? Think of your decision as if it was with a future mate.

"Can I imagine a future with you?"

Bigger Picture: Think looooooooooooonnnnnnnnnng term.

Some questions you should ask yourself:

- At what company will I be able to learn the MOST from?

- At what company will I be able to meet awesome people?

- At what company will I be able to enjoy the work I do?

- At what company would I prefer to stay at after my internship is over?

- At what company can I see a future with?

Especially when you're young, your goal should be optimizing for learning, not money.

Once you make a decision, commit for the whole internship duration.

Don't sign an offer and back out last minute. It's disrespectful and you burn a bridge between you and that recruiter.

Accept the job offer, sign the documents, and make everything official. You've earned it!

Email the other companies you interviewed with and politely inform them of your decision.

Thank them for their time and the opportunity to interview. More importantly, keep that bridge alive! You never know if you will apply to that company again or see them again at future conferences, meet ups, or networking events.

Own your internship.

During your internship, learn as MUCH as you can. Meet awesome people, build strong relationships, and most importantly... have fun! :)

If you've followed all the advice from this book, you would have chosen a position at a company that helps you learn what you want to learn with awesome people.

Congratulations.

What should I do if a company rejects me?

Thank them again and send them all your ideas. Celebrate because on the bright side, you practiced your interviewing skills and have a possible connection to the company if you ever decide to work there in the future.

FAREWELL

I really hope you use this book as a reference for all future internships or jobs you apply to. Thanks so much for reading. If this book was helpful to you, I would super appreciate a review on Amazon.

"Review on Amazon!? That means I have to get out my computer and spend one minute writing..."

Yeah, I normally don't write reviews for books either. I get it.

But now that I'm technically an "author", I actually need reviews in order for more people to find my book. Authors THRIVE on reviews! If you would be oh so kind and tell potential Amazon customers your honest opinion (good or bad), I would be super appreciative.

Here's the link that takes you straight to the review page: OutsideOfTheClassroom.com/InternshipReview

Thanks! And as always, reach out and say hi! Tell me your success story. Tell me how you celebrated after you got your internship. Let me know how I can ever help on your journey.

Your friend,

Tam

@MrTamPham

P.S. If you haven't already, go to **OutsideOfTheClassroom.com/Intern-shipBonus**, and enter in your name and email to get updates on this book, internship opportunities, and a curated list of articles and books every week to help you on your journey.

P.S.S. Thanks again for reading. I truly appreciate you.

Made in the USA
Lexington, KY
10 May 2017